CHARLIE MILLER

The Vanishing Verdict Series: Book 1 of 7

Samira, Ethan & Jonas Crime Thriller Series 1

This book was professionally typeset on Reedsy.
Find out more at reedsy.com

Contents

1

The Verdict

The air inside the packed courtroom was thick with anticipation. Reporters lined the back row, their fingers hovering over keyboards, ready to unleash headlines the moment the verdict was read. Spectators leaned forward in their seats, some whispering to one another, others clutching their coats as if bracing for impact.

Carter Langston sat at the defendant's table, unmoved. His tailored navy-blue suit was pristine, his platinum cufflinks gleaming under the fluorescent lights. Not a single strand of his salt-and-pepper hair was out of place. He exuded the quiet confidence of a man who believed himself untouchable.

The bailiff called the court to order. Judge Rebecca Holloway, an imposing woman with silver-streaked auburn hair, strode in, her black robe flowing behind her. She settled into her seat, her gaze hard as stone as she glanced at the jury.

"Ladies and gentlemen of the jury," she said, her voice echoing through the courtroom. "Have you reached a verdict?"

A short, stocky man in his fifties, the jury foreman, rose, his hands gripping the paper in front of him. He swallowed hard.

His Adam's apple bobbed like a buoy in a stormy sea.

"We have, Your Honor."

A hush fell over the room. The tension was so thick it could have been cut with a knife.

Judge Holloway nodded. "Proceed."

The foreman cleared his throat. "On the charge of first-degree murder, in the matter of the State of New York versus Carter Langston, we find the defendant... guilty."

For the first time in the grueling eight-week trial, Langston blinked. A subtle reaction, but to those watching him closely, it was the first crack in his unshakable composure. His attorney, Mitchell Dorne, inhaled sharply but said nothing. He, too, had expected a different outcome.

A ripple of reactions spread through the room. One woman gasped. Another let out a quiet sob. The families of the thirty-seven victims, seated in the first two rows, clung to one another, eyes wet with tears of relief.

Judge Holloway's gavel struck the podium. "Order!"

The courtroom silenced once more.

"Mr. Langston, please rise."

Carter Langston stood, buttoning his suit jacket as if he were preparing for a business meeting instead of receiving his fate.

"You have been found guilty of thirty-seven counts of murder," Judge Holloway continued. "Your wealth, your influence, your power—they could not shield you from justice."

Langston's eyes locked onto hers, unreadable, as if he were merely watching a particularly uninteresting television program.

"The State has recommended a sentence of life in prison without the possibility of parole." Holloway's voice didn't waver. "And this court sees no reason to rule otherwise."

A murmur rolled through the courtroom, hushed whispers of disbelief. No one had ever truly believed Langston would face the full weight of the law. Not a man of his stature. Not a man with his connections.

But today, justice had spoken.

"This court is adjourned," Judge Holloway declared, slamming her gavel once more.

The room exploded into movement. Reporters rushed for the exits, eager to file their stories. Victims' families clutched one another, their grief momentarily softened by the hard-fought victory. Prosecutors exchanged hushed, tense words with their colleagues. Langston, however, remained eerily still, his expression unreadable.

Elliot Grayson observed the scene from the press section, his heart hammering against his ribs. He had covered this trial from the beginning, had sat through the gruesome testimonies, the mounting evidence, the air-tight case that had left little doubt of Langston's guilt. And yet, something gnawed at the back of his mind—a whisper of unease, as if the story wasn't over.

He turned his gaze to Langston. The man's lips curved into the faintest hint of a smile.

It lasted less than a second, but Elliot saw it. And it sent a chill crawling down his spine.

Langston was escorted from the courtroom by two uniformed officers, his attorney trailing behind him, already whispering about appeals. The billionaire barely seemed to register them. He walked with deliberate, measured steps, his face a mask of calm control.

Elliot knew that expression. It wasn't the face of a man whose empire had just crumbled. It was the face of a man who still had a hand to play.

As the press rushed to get reactions from the prosecution team, Elliot turned to his photographer, Nina Park.

"Did you see that?"

She lowered her camera, frowning. "See what?"

"That smile."

Nina shook her head. "I was focusing on the family reactions."

Elliot exhaled sharply, running a hand through his dark hair. Maybe he was reading too much into it. Maybe Langston was just another rich sociopath who didn't know how to process defeat.

Or maybe...

"Let's get outside," he said. "I want to be there when they take him to the transport van."

Nina nodded, grabbing her gear. The two maneuvered through the crowd, weaving past spectators and journalists, the scent of stale coffee and perfume lingering in the air. As they reached the courthouse steps, the afternoon sun glared down, flashing against camera lenses.

A black armored van was parked at the curb, two uniformed marshals standing beside it. Langston emerged from a side entrance, flanked by guards, and was led down the steps. The crowd erupted into shouts—some hurling curses, others crying out for justice.

Langston didn't react. His face remained impassive as he was loaded into the van, the doors slamming shut behind him. The engine roared to life, and the vehicle rolled forward, disappearing around the corner.

Elliot watched it go, unease settling like a stone in his stomach.

He had covered hundreds of cases, witnessed dozens of convictions, but something about this one felt... wrong. There was an air of finality that was too neat, too orchestrated.

And then there was Langston's smile.

Elliot had no way of knowing it yet, but by sunrise, the trial of Carter Langston would be nothing more than a ghost. The courtroom, the judge, the jury—every piece of it would vanish as if it had never happened.

And Elliot Grayson would be the only one left who remembered.

2

Echoes of the Erased

Elliot Grayson sat frozen in his apartment, his eyes locked on the screen. The courthouse surveillance footage had played over and over, each loop confirming the impossible. At 3:07 a.m., a blank gap consumed the footage. Five minutes later, the courtroom was pristine, untouched. The judge, jury, prosecution—gone, as if they had never existed.

He clenched his fists, breathing heavily. This wasn't just tampered evidence. This was something far beyond judicial corruption. This was erasure.

His phone buzzed. A restricted number. He hesitated before answering. "Grayson."

A deep voice crackled on the line. "You're playing with fire."

Elliot straightened. "Who is this?"

"You already know." The line went dead.

Elliot stared at his phone, pulse hammering. The words weren't a threat. They were a warning.

The Vanishing Trail

Elliot stormed into the *New York Sentinel* office, past rows of desks and the usual newsroom chaos. He needed someone to confirm what he was seeing, someone who wouldn't dismiss him as insane.

Samantha Vega—his closest ally and investigative partner—was hunched over her desk, tearing through reports. He dropped a flash drive onto her keyboard.

"Tell me I'm not crazy."

Samantha arched an eyebrow but plugged the drive in. The footage played. Her frown deepened. "This is—what the hell?" She scrubbed through the missing minutes, trying different settings. "There's no glitch. This is... deliberate."

Elliot leaned closer. "Someone erased everything. Like they never existed."

Samantha rubbed her temples. "Okay. Let's assume that's true. Who has the power to do that?"

Elliot exhaled sharply. "Who benefits from Carter Langston walking free?"

The Hollow Trial

An hour later, they sat in a coffee shop across from the courthouse. Elliot's laptop was open, news reports pulled up. The headlines were staggering.

"'Billionaire Carter Langston Cleared of All Charges.'"

"'No Evidence of Trial Against Carter Langston Ever Existed.'"

"'Conspiracy Theorists Spin Fake Trial Story.'"

Elliot's fingers clenched around his coffee cup. "They're gaslighting an entire city."

Samantha clicked on an article. "The victims are still real. Their families remember. But the case files? Gone. The official arrest records? Erased. Every report that mentioned the trial? Scrubbed." She turned the screen toward him. "Except yours."

Elliot's mouth went dry. His original report still existed—on a local backup server—but everything else had been wiped.

Someone wanted him to see this.

A Witness That Shouldn't Exist

Elliot's next move was obvious: find someone who had been inside that courtroom.

He called every source he had. Dead ends. People either denied involvement or simply weren't there. But then, a name surfaced.

Angela Marin—juror number six.

Elliot and Samantha reached her address in Brooklyn by nightfall. The small house was dark, blinds drawn. Elliot knocked. No answer.

He tried again. "Ms. Marin, my name is Elliot Grayson. I'm a journalist—"

The door cracked open. A single bloodshot eye peered out. "Go away."

"I know about the trial."

The door shut. Then, after a pause, the chain rattled. The door creaked open just enough for them to slip inside.

Angela was a wreck—hair disheveled, hands trembling. "They told me to forget. But I can't."

Samantha took out her phone. "Who told you?"

Angela gripped her arm. "They're watching. They erase things. They erase people." Her voice dropped to a whisper. "I shouldn't be here."

Elliot pressed forward. "What do you remember?"

Angela's eyes darted to the window. "The trial happened. We convicted him. The evidence was undeniable. The judge read the verdict." She swallowed. "Then the lights flickered. There was... a sound. Like something breaking."

Elliot frowned. "Breaking?"

Angela hesitated, then whispered, "Like reality itself."

Samantha exchanged a glance with Elliot. This was bigger

than a cover-up.

Angela's breath hitched. "I woke up in my bed the next morning. Like the trial never happened."

Elliot's blood ran cold. "Did they threaten you?"

Angela reached for something under a cushion and handed him a small, folded piece of paper. One word was printed in bold, black ink:

LEAVE.

She swallowed hard. "I think they're coming for me next."

The Vanishing Warning

They left Angela's house in silence. The street was eerily quiet. Too quiet.

Elliot's gut twisted. "We need to get her somewhere safe."

Samantha nodded. "She's the last juror left. If they find out she talked..."

The thought was left unfinished as Angela's porch light flickered. Then the entire block went dark.

Elliot grabbed Samantha's arm. "Move. Now."

They sprinted toward their car just as a black SUV rounded the corner, headlights cutting through the darkness.

Angela's scream pierced the night.

Elliot turned back—too late. The front door swung open violently. Shadows moved inside.

Then silence.

Samantha dragged him toward the car. "We have to go. Now."

Elliot clenched his fists, every muscle screaming to turn back. But Angela was gone. **Erased.**

He threw the car into gear. "No more running. We find out who did this."

Samantha met his gaze. "And what if they come for us?"

Elliot stared at the empty house in the rearview mirror.

"They already are."

3

Shadows of Doubt

Elliot Grayson sat in the dimly lit office of *The Manhattan Tribune*, the glow of his laptop screen illuminating his furrowed brow. The newsroom hummed with the usual late-night chaos—phones ringing, reporters debating headlines, the occasional burst of laughter from the bullpen. But Elliot was trapped in a silence of his own making, drowning in the impossible case unfolding before him.

He leaned back in his chair, fingers drumming against the desk, staring at his notes. Carter Langston had been tried, convicted, sentenced. The victims had died gruesome deaths. Yet somehow, within the span of one night, the entire trial had been erased from existence. The courthouse security footage showed an empty courtroom. The judge's chambers had been cleared out as if they had never been occupied. And the jury? Twelve names that now led to ghosts.

Elliot had spent the past two days tracking them down, scouring public records, social media, and old news reports. Every trace of their existence had been scrubbed clean. Birth records, addresses, driver's licenses—gone. Even the courthouse clerks had no memory of the trial. And yet, he had the footage. He had his own reporting from the trial, now looking more like the ramblings of a madman than a credible journalist.

He rubbed his temples and reached for his coffee, now lukewarm. He needed another lead—something, anything that could tether reality back to what he knew had happened.

A ding from his laptop snapped him back to focus. An email. **No Subject. No Sender.**

He hesitated before opening it. The message was short.

"You're looking for them. Stop."

His pulse quickened. He checked the metadata—nothing. Whoever sent this knew how to cover their tracks. But if someone was warning him off, that meant he was onto something.

He grabbed his phone and dialed Naomi Carter, his editor and longtime friend. It rang twice before her familiar, no-nonsense voice came through.

"You better have something good, Grayson."

"I have something terrifying." He hesitated. "And I think I'm being watched."

A beat of silence. Then, "Where are you?"

"In the office."

"Stay there. I'm coming to you."

Twenty minutes later, Naomi stormed into his office, trench coat damp from the persistent New York drizzle. She shut the door firmly behind her, eyes scanning the room before locking onto him.

"Tell me everything," she said, dropping into the chair across from his desk.

Elliot exhaled sharply and recounted everything—the disappearing jurors, the wiped records, the mysterious email.

Naomi's expression hardened with every word. When he finished, she leaned forward, voice low and controlled.

"You think someone's tampering with reality?"

He scoffed. "You hear yourself? It sounds insane."

"But?"

He ran a hand through his hair. "But I sat through that trial, Naomi. I interviewed victims' families. I watched Langston's face when the verdict was read. And now it's like none of it happened. That's not just a cover-up—that's something else."

She nodded slowly, considering. "You said you have the footage?"

Elliot turned his laptop around and played the clip from the courthouse security feed—twelve jurors walking into the courtroom on the morning of the verdict, the judge taking his seat, Langston standing as the ruling was read aloud. He let it run for a moment before pausing.

Naomi squinted at the screen. "Where's the timestamp?"

His blood ran cold. He rewound the footage, scanned every frame. There was no timestamp. No courthouse watermark. Just a video file that, for all intents and purposes, might as well have never existed.

Naomi leaned back, arms crossed. "Someone's playing with you, Grayson."

"Then they're playing with reality itself."

The next morning, Elliot found himself parked outside an apartment complex in Queens, staring up at the window of Juror #6, a woman named Lisa Marsh. According to records—before they disappeared—she was a nurse at a local hospital, mid-thirties, lived alone.

His gut told him she was still out there. Maybe she had gone into hiding. Maybe she had sensed something was wrong before the rest of them vanished. He had to know.

He double-checked the address in his notes and stepped out of the car. The apartment building was old, brick crumbling along the edges, a rusted fire escape running up the side. The buzzer system was outdated, barely legible. He pressed #6 and waited.

No answer.

He tried again. Nothing.

Elliot frowned and took a step back. He glanced up. A light was on in her window.

Someone was home.

Instinct kicked in. He scanned the street—quiet, early morning commuters walking to the subway, a couple of dog walkers, nothing out of the ordinary. He made his way to the side of the building, where the fire escape hung just out of reach.

Sighing, he found a crate and hauled himself up. The metal groaned beneath his weight as he climbed to the third floor. When he reached Lisa's window, he hesitated.

Then he saw it.

Inside, the apartment was wrecked. Papers strewn across the floor. Couch overturned. Blood smeared along the wall.

And in the center of it all, standing completely still, was Lisa Marsh.

No, not standing.

She was **frozen**.

Elliot felt his breath hitch. Lisa was mid-step, one foot slightly raised, arms out as if she had been caught in the act of running. Her expression was one of sheer terror, mouth parted in a silent scream.

He pressed his fingers against the glass. "Lisa?"

No movement. No blinking.

It was like she had been trapped between moments.

Elliot's mind raced. He reached for his phone to snap a picture. The second he did, the room **reset**.

Lisa was gone. The apartment was spotless. No papers, no overturned couch, no blood. As if none of it had ever happened.

Elliot stumbled back against the railing, heart hammering.

Someone wasn't just erasing people. They were **rewriting time itself.**

4

Shattered Illusions

Elliot Grayson sat in the dimly lit corner of his apartment, the glow from his laptop casting sharp shadows across his face. The air was thick with tension, a mixture of disbelief and simmering paranoia. On his screen, the official records of Carter Langston's trial had vanished. No court filings. No media reports. No police records. It was as if the entire legal process had never taken place.

He leaned back, rubbing his temples. The judge, the jury, the evidence—*all gone.* How was this possible? He had witnessed the trial with his own eyes, reported on it, lived it. The victims were still dead. The families still mourning. And yet, the world acted as if nothing had ever happened.

His fingers hovered over the keyboard before typing in a different search: *Judge Benjamin Holloway.* A moment later, the screen blinked back at him: **No results found**.

Elliot's stomach twisted. Judge Holloway had presided over Langston's trial. He had sentenced the billionaire to life in prison without parole. And now, he was a ghost.

A knock at the door jolted him from his thoughts. Elliot's heart

16

hammered in his chest. He hadn't been expecting anyone. He moved cautiously toward the peephole and exhaled in relief—it was Naomi Carter, his trusted editor at the *New York Sentinel.*

He swung the door open. "Naomi, you scared the hell out of me."

She stepped inside, closing the door firmly behind her. "We need to talk."

Elliot gestured to the couch, but she remained standing, arms folded. "Elliot, I don't know what's going on, but something is wrong. The paper's archives don't have any record of your articles on the trial. I checked the backup servers, our physical records—*nothing.* The system flagged your bylines as errors, like they never existed."

Elliot's pulse quickened. "You're saying—"

"I'm saying," she interrupted, "that someone with *serious power* wants this case erased."

A heavy silence settled between them. Elliot's investigative instincts were screaming at him. This wasn't just a cover-up. This was something far more insidious.

"Naomi," he said carefully, "we need to go deeper. We need to find out who's behind this."

Naomi sighed, rubbing her forehead. "I was afraid you'd say that."

The following morning, Elliot sat in an unmarked car outside Langston Tower, the billionaire's flagship headquarters. His contact, a former security analyst named Thomas Briggs, had agreed to meet him in the underground parking garage.

Elliot drummed his fingers on the steering wheel, eyes scanning for threats. He wasn't sure who he was up against, but he knew one thing—they were watching him.

A sudden motion caught his attention. Briggs, a wiry man in his late forties, emerged from the stairwell and slid into the passenger seat. His face was pale, eyes darting nervously.

"You shouldn't have come here," Briggs muttered, pulling his coat tighter around him. "They're cleaning house. Erasing people."

Elliot clenched his jaw. "Who? Who's behind this?"

Briggs hesitated before slipping a flash drive into Elliot's hand. "This has everything I could pull before they shut me out. Bank transactions, sealed court orders, surveillance footage. If you dig deep enough, you'll find something called *The Phoenix Directive*."

Elliot frowned. "The Phoenix Directive?"

Briggs nodded. "It's some kind of project. All I know is that once you're marked by it, you cease to exist."

A chill crawled up Elliot's spine. "Marked?"

Briggs exhaled sharply. "I need to go. If they find out I spoke to you—"

A sudden, sharp *pop* echoed through the garage. Briggs jerked violently, his head snapping forward. Blood sprayed across the dashboard.

Elliot's instincts took over. He threw the car into drive and slammed his foot on the gas just as another shot shattered the back windshield. The tires screeched as he tore out of the garage, heart pounding.

In the rearview mirror, a figure dressed in black stood in the shadows, lowering a rifle.

Elliot gritted his teeth. Someone wanted this buried. And they were willing to kill to keep it that way.

He tightened his grip on the steering wheel. They had just made their biggest mistake.

They had underestimated him.

Back in his apartment, Elliot plugged the flash drive into his laptop. The files were encrypted, but he had contacts who could crack them. He picked up his phone and dialed a number.

"Lana, I need you to do something for me."

Lana Reyes, his go-to cybersecurity expert, sighed on the other end. "Elliot, the last time you said that, I ended up on a federal watchlist."

"This is bigger."

A pause. "How big?"

He glanced at the blood-stained sleeve of his jacket. "Life or death."

Silence.

"Send it over," she finally said. "And Elliot?"

"Yeah?"

"If this is as dangerous as you say, you'd better be ready to run."

Elliot exhaled slowly. He already knew that.

But there was nowhere left to run.

5

Into the Shadows

The darkness inside the storage unit was suffocating, thick with the scent of old paper, metal, and something faintly chemical. Elliot Grayson hesitated for a beat, his heart hammering in his chest as his flashlight cut through the gloom. The unit, numbered 412, had been left unlocked—just as John Kendrick had instructed. But something about the silence felt wrong.

Elliot stepped inside cautiously, his journalistic instincts screaming that this was a trap. The walls of the unit were lined with old filing cabinets, stacks of banker's boxes, and a single wooden desk pushed against the far wall. The air was stale, the dust undisturbed, except for faint drag marks on the concrete floor.

His fingers tingled as he reached out and pulled open the top drawer of the desk. A stack of manila folders sat inside, crisp despite their age. Elliot flipped through them quickly—court transcripts, bank statements, internal memos from Langston Industries. Documents that should not exist, yet here they were, detailing everything from black-market dealings to offshore accounts that linked Langston to shell companies responsible for laundering millions.

The final folder sent a shiver down his spine. It was labeled **"Verdict Manipulation: Project Vortex."**

Elliot swallowed hard, opening the folder with careful hands. Inside were pages of what looked like case notes—handwritten records of secret judicial proceedings, mentions of high-profile cases where verdicts had simply vanished from history. And then he saw it—his own name, scribbled in bold ink at the bottom of the last page.

Elliot Grayson—Active Surveillance. Status: Escalating Risk.

The world seemed to tilt. His mouth went dry. Someone had been tracking him. Watching him. And they considered him a threat.

Before he could fully process the implications, the hairs on the back of his neck rose. A creak sounded behind him. The unmistakable shift of weight on concrete. He wasn't alone.

Spinning around, he barely had time to react before a hand clamped over his mouth. A sharp, metallic scent filled his nostrils. Chloroform. His vision blurred as he thrashed against the assailant, but the strength in the grip was overwhelming. His knees buckled. The last thing he saw before darkness claimed him was the open folder on the desk—his name staring back at him like a death sentence.

Elliot came to with a gasp, his lungs burning for air. He was no longer in the storage unit. A dim, flickering fluorescent bulb illuminated the room—gray walls, a metal table, and a single chair bolted to the floor. A metal door loomed ahead, its hinges rusted but sturdy.

His wrists were zip-tied to the arms of the chair. Testing the restraints, he found them tight—whoever had brought him here wasn't taking any chances.

A voice broke the silence. **"Elliot Grayson. You just don't know when to stop, do you?"**

The figure stepped into the light. A man in a charcoal suit, lean but powerful, his eyes sharp like polished steel. **Victor Dane.** Elliot had seen his face before—Langston's personal fixer, the man who made problems disappear.

Elliot's throat was dry, but he managed a hoarse response. **"You must be running out of places to hide the bodies if you're resorting to kidnapping journalists."**

Dane smirked, tapping a manila folder against the metal table. **"We prefer to think of it as a precaution. You've been asking a lot of questions, digging where you shouldn't. And now, you've seen things you were never meant to see."**

Elliot let out a slow breath, steadying his nerves. **"You can kill me, but you can't kill the truth. I sent copies of everything I found to my editor. If I disappear, the story goes live."**

Dane tilted his head. **"Clever. But I think you overestimate how much control you have."**

He tossed the folder onto the table. **"Your editor, Mark Carlson? He resigned this morning. Apparently, he decided to take an unexpected vacation. Left the country."**

A cold dread settled in Elliot's stomach. Carlson would never abandon a story like this. Not unless he was forced to.

Dane continued, his voice smooth, methodical. **"Your files? Gone. Your credentials? Revoked. As far as the world is concerned, Elliot Grayson no longer exists."**

Elliot's pulse roared in his ears. **"You erased me."**

Dane leaned forward, his expression unreadable. **"No, Elliot. We're giving you a choice. Walk away now, and we make this all** go away. **Fight us… and you won't just vanish from journalism. You'll vanish from existence."**

Elliot forced himself to stay calm, though every instinct screamed that he was on borrowed time. **"What if I say no?"**

Dane straightened, adjusting his cufflinks. **"Then I hope you enjoy the feeling of being a ghost."**

With that, he turned and knocked twice on the metal door. It swung open, and two men in black suits stepped inside. Elliot barely had time to brace before they seized him, dragging him to his feet.

As they pulled him toward the door, Dane's voice followed like a death knell. **"Goodbye, Mr. Grayson."**

Then the world went dark again.

6

The Silent Room

Elliot Grayson sat in his car outside the dimly lit apartment complex, the rain tapping against the windshield like impatient fingers. His pulse still hadn't settled from his encounter at the courthouse—his conversation with Ava Castillo had left him shaken. The missing jurors, the erased trial, Langston's name mysteriously wiped from the system... it all pointed to something bigger than a simple case of corruption. Someone with immense power was rewriting reality itself.

He took a deep breath, refocused, and checked his phone. The message from his anonymous source still glowed on the screen: **"Apartment 3C. No cops. No backup. You want answers? Come alone."**

Elliot had spent years chasing leads, but this one felt different. It wasn't a tip-off about political scandals or corporate fraud—it was an invitation into the unknown, and something in his gut told him he was in way over his head. Still, if there was even the slightest chance that someone knew what had happened to the trial, he had to take it.

He pocketed his phone, zipped up his jacket, and stepped into the cold night. The building was an aging brownstone, its brickwork cracked, its windows thick with dust. He climbed the rusted metal stairs to the third floor, each step groaning beneath his weight. He found the door marked 3C and knocked softly.

Silence.

He tried again. **Knock. Knock.**

Still nothing.

Elliot frowned, hesitated, then cautiously tested the doorknob. It turned easily. The door creaked open to reveal a darkened apartment, the only illumination coming from the flickering streetlights outside.

"Hello?" he called, stepping inside. The air smelled stale, like old paper and something faintly metallic.

As he moved deeper into the apartment, his foot nudged something on the floor. He looked down and saw a toppled chair. His stomach tightened. Someone had been here recently—probably in a hurry.

His eyes adjusted to the darkness, revealing a cluttered living room with walls covered in newspaper clippings, photographs, and scribbled notes. It was the kind of chaotic mess he had seen in conspiracy theorists' apartments, except this one had a theme.

The Vanishing Verdict.

Every article on the wall detailed Langston's case—his arrest, his trial, his conviction. But they didn't stop there. Other cases were pinned alongside them: people accused of crimes, found guilty in court, and then suddenly... gone. No records, no appeals, no bodies.

Elliot's skin prickled. This wasn't just about Carter Langston.

Then he saw it—his own face staring back at him from a

printed photograph.

His breath caught in his throat. Someone had taken a picture of him, not long ago. He reached for it with a shaking hand. There was something written on the bottom in hurried black ink.

"You're next."

A floorboard creaked behind him.

Elliot spun, heart hammering.

A shadow darted from the kitchen. He barely had time to react before a figure lunged at him. A sharp, burning pain exploded in his side as something cold and metallic pressed against his ribs.

A knife.

He staggered backward, slamming into the wall. His attacker was fast, strong. Elliot lashed out instinctively, catching them in the shoulder. The figure grunted but didn't let go.

Desperate, Elliot grabbed the nearest object—a lamp—and swung. The ceramic base shattered against his attacker's head, sending them sprawling. He gasped, clutching his bleeding side, and stumbled toward the door.

A groggy groan rose from the floor. His attacker was already recovering. Elliot knew he wouldn't get a second chance.

He bolted into the hallway, ignoring the searing pain in his ribs. Footsteps pounded behind him. He sprinted down the stairs, bursting into the rain-slicked street. He didn't stop running until he reached his car.

He fumbled for his keys, shaking, breath coming in ragged gasps. The moment he was inside, he locked the doors, started the engine, and peeled away from the curb.

His hands trembled on the wheel. His mind raced. Who the hell was that? Who had taken his picture? And why did they think he was next?

One thing was clear: this wasn't just about a billionaire's disappearing conviction anymore.

Someone was erasing people from existence.

And now, they were coming for him.

7

Into the Abyss

The rhythmic tap of Elliot Grayson's fingers against the metal desk in his hotel room was the only sound in the dimly lit space. A single desk lamp cast shadows across the scattered documents, court records, and photographs he had pinned to the walls. The weight of what he had uncovered so far pressed heavily on his shoulders, but he knew he was still only scratching the surface of something much darker than he could have ever anticipated.

He reread the last article he had managed to publish before the Times cut him off: *Billionaire Carter Langston's trial erased— why is no one talking about it?* Yet, as he feared, the silence was deafening. Not a single major outlet had picked up on it. It was as if the world had collectively agreed to pretend the trial had never happened. But Elliot had seen the conviction, had reported on the case, had spoken to the jurors. Now, they were gone, wiped from existence. *How do you erase an entire trial?*

A sharp knock at his door pulled him out of his thoughts. He tensed. No one knew he was here—except for Valerie, his editor-turned-ally, and Michael Trent, the one detective in the NYPD who still had enough integrity to be asking the same questions. Both had promised not to show up unannounced.

Elliot reached for the Glock he had purchased after his apartment had been broken into the previous week. He approached the door cautiously, peering through the peephole. No one was there. His pulse quickened.

Another knock.

This time, he swung the door open fast, gun raised, finger on the trigger.

Nothing.

A gust of cold air rushed into the room. The hallway was empty. No footsteps. No sign of life. Elliot's grip tightened on the gun. He stepped out, glancing both ways before his eyes landed on the small envelope at his feet. Bending down, he scooped it up and re-entered the room, locking the door behind him.

He tore it open. Inside was a single sheet of paper with only two words:

Stop Digging.

No signature. No logo. Just those two words, typed in a simple, unremarkable font. He turned the envelope over, but there was nothing else. His mouth was dry. This wasn't a warning—it was a promise. He had received threats before, but this felt different. It wasn't an anonymous online message or a veiled warning from a corrupt cop. This was personal. Someone had tracked him down, knew his every move, and had the power to slip a message right under his nose without being seen.

Elliot exhaled sharply and grabbed his phone. He dialed Michael Trent, who picked up after two rings.

"Grayson?"

"Someone just left me a message outside my room. No one in the hallway. No cameras. Nothing."

Trent cursed under his breath. "Where are you?"

"Westover Hotel. Room 314."

"Stay put. I'll be there in fifteen. And Grayson—don't open the door for anyone but me."

The call ended. Elliot's grip on his phone was white-knuckled. He paced the room, waiting. Each second crawled by like an eternity. His mind raced through possibilities. Was it Langston's people? The judge? The police? Or something bigger—something beyond the scope of what even he could imagine?

Fifteen minutes passed. A knock at the door.

Elliot tightened his grip on the gun before moving toward the door. "Trent?"

"It's me. Open up."

He cracked the door just enough to confirm it was Trent before letting him in. The detective was still in his police-issued trench coat, his expression grim. He glanced at the papers spread across the room, then to the envelope Elliot handed him.

Trent read it, then exhaled through his nose. "Damn."

"That's all you got?"

Trent rubbed his temples. "Grayson, you're playing with fire. Whoever is behind this has resources, influence, and the kind of power that doesn't just threaten—you disappear."

"If you're trying to scare me, it won't work."

"Good. Because I'm not. I'm trying to keep you alive." Trent pulled out a folded piece of paper from his coat pocket and handed it to Elliot. "Recognize this?"

Elliot unfolded it and felt his stomach drop.

It was a photograph.

Taken outside the Westover Hotel.

Of him.

From tonight.

A timestamp in the corner confirmed it had been taken within the last hour. Elliot's blood ran cold. He looked up at Trent, but the detective was already speaking.

"They're watching you. And not just online. They know where you are. They know what you're doing. And they don't make empty threats."

Elliot clenched his jaw. "Then we hit them first."

Trent sighed, rubbing the bridge of his nose. "You don't get it, do you? I pulled every record I could find on Langston's case. There's nothing. Not just deleted—wiped. As in, never existed. Every name associated with it, gone."

Elliot's heartbeat pounded in his ears. "That's impossible."

"That's what I thought. Until I found this."

Trent pulled another photo from his coat and placed it on the desk. It was old, black and white, clearly decades old. It showed a courtroom—a trial in progress. A closer look at the judge, the attorneys, and the jury sent a jolt through Elliot's veins.

It was the same people from Langston's trial.

But the date on the bottom read *June 3, 1954.*

Elliot took a step back. "That's... that's not possible. They were there last week."

Trent's voice was grave. "I don't know what's going on, but whatever this is... it's been happening for a long, long time."

The room fell into a heavy silence. The walls seemed to close in, the shadows growing darker, deeper. Elliot wasn't just chasing a cover-up.

He was chasing something *impossible.*

8

Buried Echoes

Elliot Grayson had spent his career chasing shadows, but nothing compared to this. He sat at his desk, the dim glow of his laptop casting eerie silhouettes on the walls of his tiny office. Every attempt to find traces of Carter Langston's trial ended in a dead end. But what gnawed at him wasn't just the absence of records—it was the inexplicable disappearance of people who had been part of the trial. It was as if someone had reached into reality and plucked them out like weeds from a garden.

He rubbed his temples, exhaustion creeping into his bones. The digital trails of the jurors, Judge Halpern, and the prosecuting attorney had been wiped clean. Every online footprint—gone. Even archived newspaper articles covering the case had vanished. It wasn't just an erasure of records. It was a deletion of existence itself.

Elliot leaned back, staring at the ceiling. He needed something tangible, something real. Then, his mind snapped to a name. Martin Daley—the court clerk who had been present at Langston's trial. If anyone could provide answers, it was him.

The drive to Daley's house took Elliot into the quieter outskirts of Boston. The city lights faded behind him, replaced by the flickering glow of old streetlamps. When he pulled up to the address, a creeping unease settled in his gut. The house was dark, its front door slightly ajar.

Elliot hesitated before stepping out of his car. He knew better than to walk into a situation blind. He reached into his glove compartment, pulling out a small flashlight, then approached cautiously.

"Mr. Daley?" he called out, his voice barely above a whisper.

Silence.

He pushed the door open. The house smelled of dust and something metallic—coppery, sharp. Blood. Elliot's pulse quickened. He stepped inside, sweeping his flashlight across the living room. Papers were scattered across the floor, furniture overturned. A struggle had taken place here.

Then he saw it—a crimson smear trailing from the hallway to the back door.

He followed the streaks, careful with each step. The kitchen was in shambles—drawers pulled out, the fridge door left hanging open. He spotted a crumpled figure in the corner. Elliot's stomach twisted as he recognized Martin Daley's pale face, eyes wide open in frozen terror.

A message was scrawled across the floor in Daley's blood:

"STOP DIGGING."

Elliot stumbled back, bile rising in his throat. Whoever had done this wasn't just trying to silence Daley—they were sending a message. And it was meant for him.

The police arrived within minutes of Elliot's anonymous call. He stayed in the shadows as they swarmed the house. There was no way he could explain his presence without becoming a suspect himself.

He watched as detectives examined the crime scene, their hushed voices confirming what he already knew—Daley had been murdered hours ago.

Elliot retreated to his car, gripping the steering wheel as the weight of it all pressed down on him. This was bigger than he had imagined. The reach of whoever was behind Langston's vanished trial extended far beyond the courtroom.

He took a shaky breath. Someone wanted this buried. Someone powerful. But they'd made a mistake. By killing Daley, they had left behind a clue—a desperate move to silence someone who might have known too much.

Elliot pulled out his phone and scrolled through his contacts until he found a name.

Detective Rebecca Holden.

He hadn't spoken to her in years, not since she had left the force under circumstances no one dared discuss. If anyone could help him navigate this mess, it was her.

He tapped the call button.

It rang three times before she answered.

"Elliot," she said, her voice laced with suspicion. "Why the hell are you calling me?"

He exhaled sharply. "Because people are dying. And I think I just found the next body."

A beat of silence.

Then, "Where are you?"

Elliot glanced at the crime scene one last time in his rearview mirror before pulling away from the curb. "Somewhere I shouldn't be. But I have a feeling that's going to be the theme of the night."

9

The Shadow Witness

The night air in Blackwater was thick with the scent of rain-soaked asphalt, and Elliot Grayson stood outside the remnants of what was once a courthouse, now nothing more than a hollow shell of vanished history. The case files had disappeared, the judge and jury had been wiped from existence, and billionaire Carter Langston walked free, as though justice had never been served—or even attempted. Elliot had spent weeks chasing shadows, and the only thing keeping him from falling into complete despair was the nagging sensation that someone, somewhere, knew the truth. And he was close. He could feel it.

His fingers hovered over his phone. A text message had appeared from an unknown number just moments ago:

Meet me at Pier 17. Midnight. I have proof.

Elliot had learned not to ignore such messages. Too many leads had already dissolved before his eyes—witnesses who never existed, documents that never were, and a billionaire untouchable by the law. Whoever this was, they had risked enough to contact him. He had to go.

He stepped into his car, a black sedan that had already seen its fair share of reckless chases, and sped toward the docks. His pulse quickened as he neared the meeting point. The moon's reflection shimmered on the choppy waters of the bay, casting eerie ripples that distorted the already fractured world he was trying to piece together.

Pier 17 was deserted, except for a single flickering streetlamp. The wind carried the scent of salt and rust, mingled with something more acrid, something... familiar. Elliot's gut tightened. He had smelled this before—burning paper. Someone had set fire to evidence.

A shadow moved.

Elliot's grip tightened around the small voice recorder in his pocket. If he disappeared tonight, someone had to know what he had discovered. He stepped forward cautiously.

"Who's there?" His voice carried over the empty dock.

A hooded figure emerged from behind a stack of shipping containers, his face barely visible under the dim glow. The man was shaking. Whether from fear or the cold, Elliot couldn't tell.

"You're Elliot Grayson," the man said, his voice hoarse.

Elliot nodded. "And you are?"

"They call me Jonas. That's all you need to know."

Jonas pulled something from his pocket—a flash drive. "This... this is what they don't want you to see. The footage, the records... proof that Langston was convicted. Before they erased it."

Elliot reached for the drive, but Jonas yanked it back.

"They know I have it. I can't keep running. You need to take it, but you need to understand something first."

Elliot narrowed his eyes. "Understand what?"

Jonas hesitated, then exhaled sharply. "Langston... he wasn't the first. He won't be the last."

A chill ran down Elliot's spine. "What are you saying?"

Jonas' eyes darted past Elliot's shoulder. The color drained from his face. "They're here."

Elliot spun around. A black SUV, its headlights darkened, had pulled up near the pier's entrance. Silhouettes shifted inside. The hairs on the back of Elliot's neck stood up.

Jonas shoved the flash drive into Elliot's hands. "Run."

Elliot didn't need to be told twice. He bolted toward his car, heart hammering. Behind him, Jonas sprinted in the opposite direction, drawing attention away from Elliot.

Then the first gunshot rang out.

Elliot dove behind a stack of wooden crates, his breath coming in ragged gasps. Jonas let out a strangled cry, followed by a sickening thud. Elliot peered through a gap in the crates. Jonas lay sprawled on the ground, motionless. The SUV's doors swung open, and figures in black suits stepped out, scanning the dock.

Elliot clutched the flash drive tighter. Jonas had died for this.

The moment was brief—too brief. He didn't have time to mourn. He needed to move.

Keeping low, he sprinted along the pier, dodging between containers, his breath barely contained. A second shot shattered a wooden pallet inches from his head. He could hear them closing in.

Then—an opportunity. A rusted ladder led up to the scaffolding of a nearby warehouse. Without hesitation, he scrambled up, his muscles burning. He barely made it to the top before a third shot whizzed past his foot.

From the high ground, he saw his car parked near the entrance. If he could get to it, he had a chance.

He took a deep breath and jumped.

He landed hard, rolling to absorb the impact. Pain flared through his ribs, but he forced himself up. The flash drive remained clenched in his fist, his lifeline.

He sprinted to the car and yanked the door open. The engine roared to life. Tires screeched against the pavement as he peeled away from the docks, bullets ricocheting off the asphalt behind him.

He didn't stop driving until he was miles away, on an empty highway leading back into the city.

His hands trembled as he reached for his laptop. He plugged in the flash drive and waited for the files to load.

Then he saw it.

Footage of Langston's trial.

The judge. The jury. The verdict.

A courtroom that had supposedly never existed.

And then—

His own face appeared on the screen.

He wasn't in the courtroom that day.

But the footage showed him sitting right there—watching it all unfold.

Elliot's blood ran cold.

Something was very, very wrong.

10

The Vanishing Witness

Elliot Grayson sat in his dimly lit apartment, staring at the evidence board he had pieced together over the past few weeks. The faces of the vanished judge, the jury, and the missing court records stared back at him in eerie silence. Every lead he had followed so far had led to dead ends, literally. Witnesses disappeared. Files got erased. Cameras conveniently malfunctioned. It was as if someone—or something—was actively rewriting reality to bury the truth.

His phone buzzed, breaking the silence. The number was blocked. He hesitated for a moment before answering.

"Elliot," a voice whispered. It was shaky, fearful. "You need to meet me. Now."

"Who is this?"

"I don't have time. But I know what happened to Carter Langston's trial. I know why it all vanished."

Elliot shot up from his seat. "Where?"

"The old subway station on 12th and Carter Avenue. Come alone." The line went dead.

Elliot grabbed his coat and recorder, stuffing them into his messenger bag. His gut told him this could be another trap, another disappearing witness, but he had no choice. If he didn't go, the truth might slip away forever.

The subway station had been abandoned for decades, a relic of a bygone era. Rusted turnstiles stood frozen in time, and the distant echo of dripping water filled the cavernous space. Elliot stepped onto the platform, his breath visible in the cold air. The dim flickering of a lone overhead light cast long, ghostly shadows across the tiled walls.

A figure stood near the far end of the platform, wrapped in a heavy coat, hood drawn low over their face. Elliot's heartbeat quickened as he approached.

"Are you the one who called me?" he asked, keeping his distance.

The figure nodded. "I don't have long. They're watching."

"Who are they?"

The person lifted their head slightly, revealing a pair of terrified eyes. "The people who control the verdicts, the ones who erased Langston's trial."

Elliot pulled out his recorder. "Tell me everything."

The figure hesitated, glancing over their shoulder. "It started before the trial even began. Langston was never supposed to be convicted. Someone powerful ensured the entire legal process was just a performance—a show for the public."

"Who?"

"I don't know their names. No one does. But they have reach. They rewrite legal records, alter surveillance footage, erase entire lives if necessary. And when Langston was convicted, something went wrong. The script was broken. They had to reset everything."

Elliot felt a chill creep up his spine. "Reset?"

The figure nodded. "Like it never happened."

He shook his head. "That's impossible. People remember the trial. I remember it."

"They weren't able to erase everything. Some people—like you—are outliers. Maybe because you were covering the case too closely. Maybe because you saw something they couldn't erase."

Elliot's mind raced. If this was true, then his own memory was a liability. "Who are you?" he asked again.

"I worked in the courthouse. I saw the files disappear in real time. One moment they were there, the next—gone. It wasn't just digital; physical records, paper documents, everything vanished."

Elliot clenched his fists. "Why are you telling me this?"

"Because I'm next."

A noise echoed from the tunnel beyond the platform. A slow, deliberate shuffle. The figure stiffened.

"They're here."

Elliot turned, scanning the darkness. A pair of faint red lights blinked in the distance, like mechanical eyes.

"Run."

The figure shoved a flash drive into Elliot's hand before bolting toward the emergency exit stairs. Elliot was right behind them, sprinting up the cracked steps. A metallic screech rang out from below, followed by a guttural hum. The sound of something inhuman. Something hunting.

The figure reached the top first, bursting through the rusted door into the alley. Elliot followed, slamming the door shut behind him.

But when he turned around—the figure was gone.

Vanished.

Only a single, tattered glove lay on the pavement.

Elliot's breath came in sharp gasps. He clutched the flash drive in his hand, his fingers trembling. Whatever was on it, people had died for it. And now, they would be coming for him next.

His only hope was to uncover the truth before they erased him too.

11

The Phantom Witness

Elliot Grayson sat in the dim glow of his apartment, the city humming beyond his window. The evidence—what little he had—was spread out on his coffee table. The case files, the blurred courthouse footage, the enigmatic call from Senator Alden, and the threatening warning he had received. Pieces of a puzzle that refused to fit together.

His phone buzzed. A blocked number.

He hesitated, then answered. "Grayson."

A distorted voice crackled through the speaker. "Do you want the truth, or do you want to live?"

Elliot's pulse spiked. "Who is this?"

"Meet me at Pier 17. Warehouse 6. Midnight. Alone."

The call ended.

A trap? Likely. But Elliot had spent his career following leads into danger, and this was no different. He had to know who was orchestrating the vanishing of an entire trial. He grabbed his jacket, slipped his handgun into its holster—an illegal but necessary precaution—and stepped into the night.

The docks were empty, save for the rhythmic lapping of water against the piers. Fog slithered across the pavement, curling around the warehouses like ghostly fingers. Warehouse 6 loomed ahead, its rusting metal door slightly ajar.

Elliot approached cautiously. His right hand hovered near his gun. He pushed the door open and stepped inside. A single overhead bulb buzzed, casting long, flickering shadows across the concrete floor. A figure stood at the far end, wrapped in an overcoat, a hood obscuring their face.

"You came," the figure said, voice gravelly, as if unused for years.

"You gave me a choice," Elliot countered. "Truth or survival. I want the truth."

A dry chuckle. "Then you'll die. But at least you'll die knowing."

The figure reached into their coat. Elliot's hand went for his gun—but instead of a weapon, the stranger pulled out a worn leather folder and tossed it onto a crate between them. Elliot hesitated, then flipped it open.

Inside were grainy black-and-white surveillance photos. A familiar face stared back at him.

Judge Theodore Henshaw.

Only, the timestamp on the photos was from two nights ago— twenty-four hours after the judge had supposedly vanished from existence.

Elliot's breath hitched. "This is impossible. He's gone. Every record of him erased. Every witness intimidated into silence."

"Records lie," the stranger murmured. "People don't."

Elliot thumbed through the photos. Different locations. A dark sedan. A motel. A meeting in a nondescript diner. The judge wasn't just alive—he was active.

"Where were these taken?" Elliot demanded.

"Upstate. A small town called Greystone."

Greystone. A dot on the map, barely worth a mention. Why would a high-profile judge hide out in a place like that?

"Why are you showing me this?" Elliot asked, his gaze snapping back to the stranger.

"Because they're watching me too," the figure said. "And my time is running out."

Elliot's gut tightened. "Who are 'they'?"

The stranger exhaled sharply, glancing toward the door. "The people who made Langston's trial disappear. The people who own the courts, the police, the press. You think this is just about one case? This is a system. A machine that erases anything that threatens its control."

A sharp noise outside. A scuffle of footsteps on gravel.

The stranger stiffened. "You were followed."

Elliot spun, gun raised. The warehouse door creaked open, revealing two figures in dark suits. They moved with trained precision, hands at their waists, eyes scanning the shadows.

"Mr. Grayson," one of them said, voice calm, rehearsed. "We need you to come with us."

"Not happening," Elliot said, tightening his grip on the gun.

"You misunderstand." The agent smiled coldly. "This isn't a request."

The stranger beside him moved fast—too fast. In a blur, they grabbed the leather folder, shoved it into Elliot's hands, and whispered, "Run."

Then, in a single, practiced motion, the stranger pulled a concealed knife and lunged.

Elliot bolted as chaos erupted behind him. The wet thunk of a blade meeting flesh. A strangled grunt. The crack of a gunshot.

He sprinted through the side door, feet pounding against the dock. Behind him, voices shouted. More gunfire. The night swallowed the sound.

He ducked behind a shipping container, heart hammering. He risked a glance back. The stranger was gone. So were the men in suits.

And so was the evidence.

Except for what he held in his shaking hands.

He exhaled sharply. He was running out of time. If Judge Henshaw was alive, if the trial had been erased by something bigger than he could comprehend—he needed to get to Greystone. Now.

Without looking back, he ran toward his car. Toward the truth.

Toward the next step in unraveling the vanishing verdict.

12

Whispers in the Dark

Elliot Grayson sat in his car outside the derelict warehouse, his fingers drumming a nervous rhythm against the steering wheel. The night was suffocatingly silent, the kind that made even the city's usual background noise feel eerily absent. He double-checked his phone—still no service. It was as if the universe itself conspired to keep this meeting off the record.

The message had been cryptic: *You want the truth? Come alone. Midnight. Pier 17.*

Every instinct screamed at him to turn around, but instincts hadn't gotten him this far. Facts had. And right now, the facts weren't adding up. He had spent days unraveling the impossible—Carter Langston's conviction erased, the jurors missing, the judge gone. The world had moved on as if the trial had never existed. But it had. He knew it.

And now, someone else knew it too.

He stepped out of the car, the cold seeping through his thin jacket. The distant hum of the harbor was the only sound breaking the stillness. His eyes scanned the area—rusted shipping containers, a skeletal crane, and beyond it, the endless black expanse of the water. No signs of movement.

A shadow detached from the darkness.

Elliot's muscles tensed. The figure approached cautiously, a hood drawn low over their face. "You alone?" the voice was distorted, like they were speaking through clenched teeth.

"You asked me to be."

The figure exhaled sharply, then jerked their head toward the warehouse. "Inside. Too exposed here."

Elliot hesitated for only a second before following. The warehouse door groaned as it swung open, revealing a cavernous space filled with abandoned crates and the overwhelming stench of mildew. A single hanging bulb flickered overhead, casting elongated, shifting shadows.

The figure pulled back their hood, revealing a gaunt, pale face. Dark eyes darted around as if expecting danger from every direction. "You're digging too deep," the man whispered. "They're watching you."

Elliot's pulse quickened. "Who?"

A bitter smile played on the man's lips. "You think Langston was the mastermind? He was just the pawn. The real power—the ones who *erased* him—they don't leave loose ends."

A chill raced down Elliot's spine. "Then why are you here?"

The man reached into his coat and pulled out a flash drive. "This has everything. The trial, the cover-up, the names."

Elliot reached for it, but the man pulled back. "Once you see this, there's no going back."

A crash from outside.

The man flinched. "They're here."

Elliot barely had time to process the words before the warehouse lights cut out completely, plunging them into darkness.

Footsteps echoed. Heavy. Purposeful.

"Run." The man shoved the flash drive into Elliot's hand before bolting toward the back exit.

Elliot didn't wait to see who was coming. He sprinted in the opposite direction, ducking behind a stack of crates just as the warehouse door burst open. Flashlights swept through the space. Shadows moved like wraiths against the walls.

A gunshot rang out. A strangled gasp. Then silence.

Elliot clamped a hand over his mouth, his heart pounding so hard he feared they'd hear it. Footsteps approached, slow and methodical. A voice, deep and calm, cut through the darkness.

"Mr. Grayson, we know you're here. Hand it over, and this ends tonight."

His grip tightened around the flash drive. No. Not like this.

The footsteps stopped just feet away. The beam of a flashlight passed over his hiding spot, pausing for a fraction of a second before moving on. They didn't see him.

Not yet.

Elliot's breath came in shallow, controlled bursts. His mind raced. He had seconds to decide.

Fight. Flee. Or vanish—just like the case itself.

13

The Phantom Witness

Elliot Grayson sat in his dimly lit motel room, staring at the collection of files scattered across the bed. The weight of what he had uncovered pressed against his chest like an iron vice. Every path, every lead, seemed to vanish just as he got close. But tonight, something was different. A cryptic email had arrived in his inbox an hour ago:

"Meet me at Pier 17. Midnight. Alone. Justice has a memory, even if the world does not."

The sender was anonymous. No IP trace, no name, no reply option. Just the message.

Elliot knew it could be a setup. He also knew he couldn't afford to ignore it.

The docks were eerily quiet, save for the rhythmic lapping of water against the pilings. Fog rolled in thick, swallowing the streetlights and turning them into dull orbs of orange haze. Elliot zipped up his jacket, his breath forming faint wisps in the cold night air. He stepped onto the wooden planks of Pier 17, the creaking beneath his boots the only sound.

Then, movement.

A shadow peeled away from the fog. A woman. Her hood was pulled low, concealing most of her face, but the tension in her posture was unmistakable. Elliot's fingers brushed against the pocket of his coat where his recorder lay hidden.

"You came," she said, her voice barely above a whisper.

"I don't have a habit of ignoring potential sources." Elliot kept his stance casual, but every muscle in his body was wound tight. "Who are you?"

"A mistake," she murmured. "A ghost in a world that doesn't believe in ghosts."

Elliot frowned. "Not cryptic at all. Let's try again. Who are you?"

She exhaled sharply, glancing over her shoulder before stepping closer. "My name doesn't matter. What matters is that I was in that courtroom. I saw the verdict. I saw Carter Langston sentenced. I saw the judge, the jury... the evidence. And then—"

"It was gone," Elliot finished. "Like it never happened."

She nodded. "But I remember. I remember everything."

Elliot studied her, his pulse quickening. If she was telling the truth, she was the only verifiable witness left. "Why haven't you come forward?"

Her eyes darted to the darkness behind them. "Because they know I remember. And they're watching."

A shiver crawled down Elliot's spine. "Who is 'they'?"

She shook her head. "I don't know. But they erased an entire trial like it was nothing. What do you think they'll do to me?"

Elliot had no answer.

She reached into her pocket and pulled out a small, battered flash drive. "Everything I could gather. It's not much, but it's something."

He hesitated for a fraction of a second before taking it. Their fingers brushed, and he felt how cold her hands were. Fear was an icy thing.

"Leave town," she whispered. "If you're smart, you'll walk away."

"I've never been accused of that."

A humorless smile flickered across her lips. "Then be careful, Elliot Grayson. Because when they realize you're getting too close... you'll disappear too."

A gust of wind kicked up, and for a moment, the fog thickened. When it cleared, she was gone.

Back in his motel room, Elliot plugged the flash drive into his laptop. His heart pounded as he opened the first file. A video. He clicked play.

The grainy security footage showed the courtroom on the day of the verdict. The judge sat at his bench, the jury in place, Carter Langston standing before them in an orange jumpsuit. The timestamp in the corner was correct. The verdict was read, the sentence passed.

Then, the footage glitched.

Not just a distortion. A complete wipe. The judge, the jury, the courtroom—all disappeared in an instant. The screen flickered and reloaded. Now, it was empty. A courtroom devoid of life, as though the trial had never taken place.

Elliot's hands clenched into fists. This was proof. Someone had manipulated reality itself. But how?

A noise outside made him freeze.

Footsteps. Slow. Measured. Right outside his door.

Elliot reached for his phone and started recording as he grabbed the flash drive, shoving it into his pocket. The motel's weak lock wouldn't hold if someone wanted in badly enough.

A shadow crossed the gap beneath his door.

Then, a soft knock.

Elliot didn't move.

Another knock. Louder.

He swallowed hard. Whoever was out there wasn't here for a friendly visit.

His laptop screen flickered. The video file distorted and disappeared, replaced by a flashing message:

STOP DIGGING.

The power in the motel room went out.

Elliot bolted for the window.

14

The Silent Witness

Elliot Grayson parked his car two blocks away from the old courthouse, his fingers tapping anxiously on the steering wheel. The weight of the case pressed down on him like an iron shackle. Carter Langston's trial had been erased from existence, but Elliot had found the crack in the façade—a single witness who might hold the key to unraveling this impossible conspiracy.

Her name was Lorraine Becker. A retired court stenographer, Lorraine had been present throughout Langston's trial. If anyone had a record of what had transpired before reality itself was rewritten, it would be her. But Lorraine had vanished from public records just like the trial. No address, no phone number, no trace of her existence beyond a faint paper trail leading to an old assisted living home in the suburbs.

Elliot stepped out into the cool night air, zipping up his jacket as he made his way toward the entrance. The building loomed before him, a relic of past decades with faded brick walls and dimly lit windows. A single overhead lamp flickered, casting erratic shadows across the parking lot. He hesitated, feeling the strange sensation that he was being watched. Shaking off the paranoia, he walked inside.

The lobby was eerily quiet. A tired-looking nurse sat behind the reception desk, her eyes glued to an old television playing a late-night news broadcast. She barely glanced at him as he approached.

"Excuse me," Elliot said, keeping his voice low. "I'm looking for Lorraine Becker. She used to work as a court stenographer."

The nurse's eyes flickered with recognition, but her expression quickly hardened. "No visitors after hours."

"I won't take long," Elliot pressed. "It's important."

She sighed, tapping at her keyboard. "She doesn't get many visitors. Room 312. End of the hall."

Elliot nodded his thanks and walked briskly down the dimly lit corridor. His footsteps echoed unnaturally, the silence stretching like an oppressive force. The entire place felt... wrong. As if the air itself resisted his presence. He reached Room 312 and knocked gently.

No answer.

He tried again, a little louder this time. Still nothing. His gut twisted. Something wasn't right.

Elliot tested the doorknob—it turned easily. Pushing the door open, he stepped inside. The room was modest, furnished with a small bed, a wooden dresser, and a chair near the window. But Lorraine wasn't there.

What was there, however, made his blood run cold.

On the nightstand sat a single sheet of paper, its edges crisp as if it had been placed there moments ago. Elliot's name was scrawled across the top in trembling handwriting. His hands shook as he picked it up.

They know you're here. Leave now. Before they make you

disappear too.

A sudden noise behind him made Elliot whirl around, his heart pounding. The closet door creaked open an inch. The room's dim light barely illuminated the narrow gap, but he could see movement—someone was in there.

Elliot took a slow step forward. "Lorraine?"

Silence.

He reached out and yanked the closet door fully open.

Lorraine Becker stood inside, trembling, her wide eyes filled with terror. Her frail hands clutched a battered leather notebook to her chest as if it were the only thing keeping her grounded in reality.

Elliot exhaled in relief. "Lorraine, I—"

She cut him off with a shaky whisper. "They're coming."

His pulse spiked. "Who? Who's coming?"

Lorraine shoved the notebook into his hands. "Take this and run. Don't stop. Don't look back."

Elliot hesitated, but then he heard it—a slow, deliberate creak of footsteps in the hallway. Someone was approaching. Lorraine's panic was infectious, and Elliot's survival instincts kicked in. He stuffed the notebook into his jacket, grabbed Lorraine's wrist, and pulled her toward the door.

The hallway was empty, but the feeling of being watched was suffocating. Elliot steered Lorraine toward the back exit, but before they could reach it, the overhead lights flickered and died, plunging the corridor into darkness.

Then came the whispering.

It was faint at first, like wind rustling through leaves, but it grew in intensity—urgent, distorted voices speaking in a language Elliot couldn't understand. He tightened his grip on Lorraine's hand, his breath coming fast and shallow. He didn't need to understand the words to know what they meant.

Run.

Elliot yanked Lorraine forward, sprinting down the hall, guided only by the dim green glow of an emergency exit sign. The whispers turned into a cacophony of sound, like a hundred voices screaming in unison. Lorraine sobbed beside him, struggling to keep pace.

The exit door was just ahead.

And then it slammed shut.

Elliot skidded to a halt. The door had moved on its own. No wind, no visible force. Just an undeniable, terrifying finality.

A shadow loomed in the darkness behind them. A tall, indistinct figure, its features blurred as though reality itself refused to acknowledge its presence. It raised one hand, and the whispering stopped.

Silence. Oppressive. Complete.

Lorraine gasped as her body went rigid. Her eyes widened in horror, her lips parting in a silent scream. Elliot barely had time to react before she crumpled to the floor, unmoving.

Elliot's own body felt sluggish, his limbs tingling as though something unseen was trying to unravel him from existence. He fought against it, against the heavy pull of whatever force had taken Lorraine.

With a final burst of energy, he lunged for the notebook in his jacket. If nothing else, he had to get it out of here. He had to expose the truth.

As his fingers curled around it, the lights flickered back on.

The hallway was empty.

Lorraine was gone.

Not dead. Not unconscious. Just... gone.

Elliot staggered backward, the notebook clutched tightly in

his shaking hands. He turned and ran, bursting through the emergency exit into the night air. He didn't stop running until he reached his car, his breath coming in ragged gasps.

He had Lorraine's notebook. He had proof.

But at what cost?

As he drove away, his rearview mirror reflected nothing but darkness behind him. And somewhere, deep in the recesses of his mind, the whispers had not entirely stopped.

15

Shadows in the Mirror

Elliot Grayson sat in his dimly lit apartment, staring at the case files scattered across his coffee table. The weight of the investigation pressed down on him like an invisible force. Carter Langston's erased trial was no longer just a story—it was an abyss pulling him deeper into a reality where truth itself could be rewritten. His fingers tapped rhythmically against his whiskey glass as he replayed the events of the past week in his mind.

The door to his apartment was locked, yet there was a faint creak from the hallway. Elliot tensed. He reached for the Glock he kept beneath the couch, his senses heightened. He moved silently, pressing his back against the wall beside the door. Another creak. Someone was there.

With measured control, he twisted the knob and yanked the door open, gun aimed. But there was no one.

Instead, a small white envelope lay on the floor. No return address. Just his name written in sharp, bold letters.

Elliot scanned the hallway. Empty. The overhead fluorescent lights buzzed ominously. He bent down, picked up the envelope, and shut the door behind him, locking it securely.

He took a seat and examined the envelope. The handwriting was precise, almost too perfect, as if it had been mechanically printed rather than handwritten. He tore it open and unfolded the single sheet of paper inside.

You were never supposed to find out.

His pulse quickened. No signature. No explanation. Just six words, yet they carried the weight of a death sentence. He knew intimidation tactics when he saw them. This wasn't a warning. It was a statement of fact.

Elliot pulled out his phone and dialed Detective Sarah Whitmore. She picked up on the second ring.

"Grayson, you have a lead?"

"I just got a message. No return address. Just says, 'You were never supposed to find out.'"

There was a brief silence. Then, "You alone?"

"Yes."

"I'm coming over."

Twenty minutes later, Sarah knocked on his door. Elliot let her in, handing her the note. She examined it with furrowed brows, then placed it in an evidence bag from her pocket.

"This paper—it's high-quality, specialized stock. Whoever sent this has resources," she noted. "And they're watching you."

Elliot exhaled, running a hand through his hair. "That's not the worst part. I checked the surveillance cameras in the hallway."

Sarah looked up. "And?"

"There's no footage of anyone leaving the note. It just... appeared."

Sarah's face hardened. "That's impossible."

Elliot walked over to his laptop and played the footage. The hallway remained empty. One second, the floor was bare. The next, the envelope was there.

Sarah folded her arms. "I don't like this. Someone's screwing with you. The only question is—how?"

Before Elliot could answer, his phone buzzed. Unknown number.

He hesitated, then answered. "Who is this?"

A voice—distorted, metallic—spoke: "Stop digging, Grayson. Or you'll vanish next."

The line went dead.

Sarah grabbed his phone, trying to trace the number. "Burner. No signal trace."

Elliot clenched his jaw. "They're escalating."

Sarah nodded. "And that means we're getting close."

Elliot turned to the files on his desk, flipping through pages of redacted testimonies, missing evidence logs, and the jury list. One name stood out—James Calloway. A juror who had supposedly vanished along with the others.

But Elliot had found something the world wasn't supposed to see. Calloway's name had appeared on a hospital admission record two nights ago. If he was alive, he was a loose end.

"We need to find Calloway," Elliot said. "Before they do."

Sarah nodded. "Then let's move."

They left the apartment, neither noticing the reflection in the mirror—a shadowy figure standing where Elliot had just been, watching as they walked away.

16

The Labyrinth of Lies

Elliot Grayson sat in his dimly lit apartment, the glow from his laptop screen reflecting off his tense features. The more he dug into Carter Langston's case, the more the threads unraveled into something impossible—something beyond corruption or legal manipulation. It was as if reality itself was shifting, erasing traces of truth before he could fully grasp them.

He clicked open an email he had received minutes ago, the sender unknown. The subject line read: **"The Witness Who Never Was."**

His pulse quickened as he opened the attachment. A blurry surveillance image loaded—grainy, but clear enough to make out figures. It showed a courtroom, unmistakably from Langston's trial. But something was off. The jurors' seats were empty. The judge's bench vacant. In their place sat a lone figure—a woman in a dark suit, standing in the center of the room, facing forward as if staring straight at the camera.

Elliot leaned in closer, heart hammering. He had never seen her before. Who was she?

A knock at his door jolted him out of his trance. He jumped, his laptop almost slipping from his lap. Glancing at the time, he saw it was just past midnight.

Another knock. Harder this time.

Cautiously, he moved toward the door, every nerve in his body on edge. "Who is it?" he called out.

Silence.

He glanced at the peephole but saw nothing but darkness. Every instinct screamed at him to step back, but against better judgment, he unlatched the lock and slowly cracked the door open.

No one was there.

Except for a single envelope, placed precisely at the threshold.

Elliot reached down, hesitated, then snatched it up. His hands trembled slightly as he tore it open. Inside was a single Polaroid photograph. He pulled it out and flipped it over.

His blood ran cold.

It was the same woman from the surveillance footage. But this time, the image was in color, clearer. And in her eyes, there was something eerie—a knowing look. Below the image, scrawled in red ink, were three words:

Find Me. Now.

Elliot wasted no time. He grabbed his car keys, shoved his laptop into his bag, and sprinted down the stairs of his apartment building. The streets of Easton Harbor were deserted at this hour, shadows stretching unnaturally beneath the flickering streetlights. His mind raced as he replayed everything he had uncovered so far—Langston's vanished trial, the missing jury, and now this phantom witness.

Who was she? And why was she reaching out now?

As he sped through the quiet city, he pulled out his phone and dialed the one person he trusted with secrets this big—Detective Marcus Holloway. The call rang four times before a groggy voice answered.

"Grayson, do you have any idea what time it is?"

"Marcus, listen to me. I just got a lead—something big."

A sigh. "Do you ever sleep?"

"No time for that. I need you to meet me at the old court-house."

Silence, then a begrudging, "Give me fifteen minutes."

Elliot hung up and tightened his grip on the steering wheel. The old courthouse had been shut down for years, replaced by a newer, sleeker judicial building. But something told him that if this woman wanted to be found, that was where he needed to go.

The courthouse loomed in the darkness, its grand pillars casting long shadows across the abandoned steps. The building had an eerie stillness, the kind that made the hairs on the back of his neck stand up.

A car pulled up behind him. Holloway stepped out, rubbing his face as if trying to wake up. "Alright, Grayson. What's so damn urgent?"

Elliot held up the Polaroid. "Do you recognize her?"

Holloway took the photo, squinting at it. "Never seen her before. Who is she?"

"That's what I'm trying to find out. But she was there, Marcus. At Langston's trial. The one that disappeared."

Holloway's expression darkened. "Are you telling me there's a witness to a trial that doesn't officially exist?"

"That's exactly what I'm telling you. And she wants me to

find her."

Holloway exhaled, rubbing his temples. "You're going to get yourself killed one of these days."

Elliot pushed forward, leading the way up the courthouse steps. The door was locked, but the side entrance—where deliveries used to come in—was slightly ajar.

"This shouldn't be open," Holloway muttered.

"Exactly," Elliot said, stepping inside.

The interior was dark, the air thick with dust and the faint scent of old paper. Their footsteps echoed eerily through the empty halls. The main courtroom was straight ahead, the heavy double doors slightly ajar.

Elliot swallowed hard and pushed them open.

The room was just as it appeared in the surveillance image. Empty jury seats. An abandoned judge's bench. And in the center, as if waiting for them, stood the woman from the photograph.

She didn't look afraid. If anything, she looked...prepared.

"Elliot Grayson," she said, her voice even, measured.

"Who are you?" he demanded.

A small smile. "You wouldn't believe me if I told you."

Holloway stepped forward, his hand near his holster. "Try us."

The woman exhaled and took a step closer. "Carter Langston was convicted in this very courtroom. I testified against him. And then..." She hesitated. "I was supposed to disappear, just like the trial. But something went wrong."

Elliot's mind reeled. "What do you mean, 'supposed to disappear'?"

She glanced around as if expecting someone—or something—to interrupt. "You don't understand what you're dealing with.

There are forces in play far beyond the law, beyond reason itself. Someone is rewriting history, erasing entire events as if they never happened."

Holloway stiffened. "That's impossible."

The woman smiled again, but this time, it held no warmth. "Is it? Then tell me, Detective—why are we standing in a courtroom that doesn't exist?"

Elliot felt the weight of her words settle in his chest. This wasn't just corruption. This was something bigger. Something unnatural.

And they were right in the middle of it.

17

The Courtroom That Never Was

Elliot Grayson's breath came in shallow gasps as he pressed himself against the cold brick wall outside the courthouse's rear entrance. The building loomed above him, its shadow stretching long beneath the dim glow of the streetlights. He had been here before—many times. He had walked these halls, documented trials, and chased justice within these walls. But tonight, he was breaking in.

The courthouse was supposed to be closed, yet a low hum of electricity thrummed through the building. It wasn't abandoned, not entirely. Someone was inside, and that only fueled Elliot's determination. He had spent the last forty-eight hours piecing together the puzzle, and every lead pointed back here—to the courtroom that supposedly never existed.

Pulling the hood of his jacket lower over his face, he checked his surroundings one last time before slipping through the rusted side door he had jimmied open earlier. A musty, sterile scent filled the air as he moved down the corridor, past empty offices with desks that hadn't been touched in years. His fingers trailed along the walls, feeling for something—anything—that didn't belong.

He knew what he was looking for.

Project Obsidian.

The name had appeared in redacted documents, whispered by terrified sources, and hinted at in the wreckage of erased lives. He had seen it scrawled in a trembling hand by the now-dead juror who had barely managed to flee before she was silenced. And now, Elliot was standing in the belly of the beast, chasing ghosts.

He found the stairs leading down to the basement level, his heart pounding. The air grew thick, damp, the temperature dropping as he descended. He reached a steel door at the bottom, the kind that belonged in a bunker, not a courthouse. There was no handle, just a keypad and a small slot for a keycard.

His hand reached into his pocket, fingers brushing against the plastic of the stolen access card he had lifted from a former court clerk who had sworn he had never worked there. He hesitated only a second before swiping it. A green light flickered, and the lock clicked open.

Inside, rows of filing cabinets lined the walls, each marked with coded numbers and cryptic initials. At the center of the room sat a single desk with an old computer monitor, its screen casting an eerie glow. Elliot moved quickly, searching for any sign of the erased case.

Then he saw it.

A metal drawer labeled: **C. Langston**.

Elliot yanked it open.

Empty.

His fingers curled into fists as frustration roiled in his chest. They had erased everything. But then, he noticed the faint imprint of paper dust. Something had been here recently.

He turned his attention to the computer. The login screen demanded credentials. He tapped the keyboard, entering an old access code he had uncovered from a disgraced prosecutor's files. To his shock, the system let him in.

A list of archived cases flickered onto the screen, file names scrambled with seemingly random characters. But as he scrolled, one caught his attention:

Trial 237-Omega: Expunged.

Expunged.

Elliot clicked on it. The screen flashed, and suddenly, lines of code scrolled rapidly, almost as if the system was fighting against him. Then, a single phrase appeared before the monitor shut down entirely:

"YOU WERE WARNED."

The room plunged into darkness.

Elliot's blood ran cold. Someone knew he was here.

He turned to run, but the steel door slammed shut with a loud clang. A red light blinked on the wall. A security lockdown. Panic clawed at his throat as he tried to pry it open, but it wouldn't budge.

Then, footsteps. Slow. Measured. Coming from the hallway outside.

Elliot pressed himself against the shelves, heart hammering as the lock disengaged with a mechanical whirr. The door creaked open, and a shadow filled the doorway.

"Mr. Grayson."

The voice was smooth, deliberate, with an edge of familiarity. As the figure stepped forward, the dim emergency light illuminated a face Elliot had seen before, though he never expected to see it here.

Judge Rebecca Holloway.

But that was impossible. She had vanished. Erased.

"Surprised?" she asked, her gaze calm, assessing. "You shouldn't be. You're meddling in something far bigger than you realize."

Elliot struggled to find his voice. "They said you were gone. No records, no past. As if you never existed."

A ghost of a smile crossed her lips. "And yet, here I am."

He took a step forward. "Where is the Langston case? The real records. What is Project Obsidian?"

Her expression darkened. "You're in over your head, Elliot. This isn't just about a trial. It's about control. The power to rewrite history, to alter reality itself."

Elliot's mind raced. "Langston's trial was real. I was there. I saw the verdict."

Holloway nodded. "And now, it never happened."

A chill ran down his spine. "Who's behind this?"

She exhaled, the weight of something unspoken hanging between them. "People you don't want to cross."

Elliot clenched his fists. "Then why are you here?"

For the first time, uncertainty flickered in her eyes. "Because there are some things even they can't erase."

She reached into her coat pocket and pulled out a small flash drive. "This is the last piece of proof. Take it and run."

Elliot hesitated before grabbing it. "What's on here?"

But before she could answer, the sound of heavy boots filled the corridor. She tensed, her face tightening with urgency. "Go. Now."

He took a step back. "What about you?"

She gave a small, sad smile. "I was erased a long time ago."

The footsteps were getting closer. Elliot turned, heart pounding as he sprinted through the room, weaving between cabinets and shelves. A gunshot rang out, the bullet striking the metal inches from where he had stood. He didn't look back.

He reached the emergency exit door on the far end of the basement and shoved it open, bursting into the cool night air. He ran until his lungs burned, until the courthouse was just another shadow in the city skyline.

Only then did he dare to look down at the flash drive clutched in his hand.

He had the truth.

But was the world ready for it?

18

The Dead Man Calls

The phone rang once. Then twice. Elliot Grayson hesitated before answering. The number was blocked, but he had learned long ago that some calls couldn't be ignored.

He pressed the phone to his ear. "Grayson."

A distorted voice came through the line, crackling with interference. "You think you know the truth? You have no idea."

Elliot's breath caught. The voice was familiar, yet impossible.

"Langston?" he whispered.

A brief silence. Then, "They lied to you. You're chasing ghosts. Meet me at the old freight yard. Midnight."

The line went dead.

Elliot sat frozen. Carter Langston had been found dead, his corpse lying in an abandoned warehouse. He had seen the autopsy photos. He had confirmed the death certificate. And yet, Langston had just called him.

The journalist's instincts screamed at him: This is a trap.

But if it wasn't? If there was even the slightest chance Langston was alive, it could blow the entire conspiracy wide open.

Elliot spent the next few hours preparing. He tucked a recorder into his pocket, checked the battery on his backup phone, and slipped a small pistol into his ankle holster. He wasn't taking any chances.

By the time he reached the freight yard, the moon was high, casting eerie shadows over the rusting train cars. The place had been abandoned for years, its silence unnerving. Elliot scanned the area, heart pounding.

A faint sound echoed through the night—the crunch of gravel beneath a footstep.

He turned sharply. "Who's there?"

A shadow stepped forward from between two rusted cargo containers.

Elliot's breath hitched. The man before him wore a dark coat and a hood, but even in the dim light, there was no mistaking the sharp angles of his face.

Carter Langston.

"You're supposed to be dead," Elliot said, voice tight.

Langston gave a wry smile. "That's what they want you to think."

Elliot's mind raced. He needed to verify this was really Langston, not an imposter. "Prove it," he said.

Langston sighed and reached into his coat. Elliot's fingers twitched toward his ankle holster, but Langston only pulled out a silver pen. He clicked it twice.

Elliot stiffened. He had seen that pen before.

"Judge Holloway gave this to me after the trial ended," Langston said. "Said I'd need something to sign my last statement before they hauled me away."

Elliot's blood ran cold. That wasn't in any public records. No one else could have known that detail.

"So what happened?" Elliot asked. "How are you standing here?"

Langston exhaled slowly. "They buried the case—literally. Erased everything. And me? They needed me gone but couldn't risk a body being found too soon. So they staged a death, planted a corpse, and kept me locked away. Until I escaped."

Elliot narrowed his eyes. "Who are 'they'?"

Langston hesitated. Then, in a low voice, he said, "Project Obsidian."

Elliot stiffened. The name matched the classified files he had found in the abandoned courthouse. A covert initiative that altered historical records, erasing entire trials from existence.

"Who runs it?" Elliot demanded.

Langston shook his head. "That's the part I never figured out. But they control everything. Judges, law enforcement, the media. If they want something erased, it's gone."

Elliot's pulse pounded. He had spent weeks chasing ghosts, trying to piece together fragments of a trial that had been wiped from existence. And now, standing before him was proof that it wasn't just the trial that had been erased—but the people involved as well.

"Why reach out to me?" Elliot asked.

Langston's expression hardened. "Because you're the only one who hasn't been silenced yet. And I need you to expose them before they come for you."

A sudden noise—a scuffle of feet on gravel. Elliot turned just in time to see movement behind the train cars.

"Run!" Langston shouted.

Gunfire erupted.

Elliot dove behind a stack of wooden pallets, bullets splintering the air. Langston bolted toward an old maintenance shed, but more figures emerged from the darkness, cutting him off.

Elliot pulled his pistol, fired blindly in the direction of the attackers. He heard one of them grunt, followed by a muffled curse.

Langston tried to double back, but two men grabbed him, dragging him toward a black SUV parked near the yard's exit.

"No!" Elliot shouted, charging forward.

A figure turned, raising a weapon. A sharp pain tore through Elliot's shoulder, knocking him back. His vision blurred as he hit the ground.

Through the haze of pain, he saw Langston struggling, kicking wildly as the operatives shoved him into the SUV. The tires screeched as the vehicle sped away into the night.

Elliot groaned, gripping his bleeding shoulder. He fumbled for his phone, hands slick with sweat. He had just gotten the biggest breakthrough of his career—and now it was slipping away.

He had to move. Had to act before Langston disappeared again—this time for good.

Gritting his teeth, he forced himself to stand.

And then, just as he reached for his phone, it vibrated.

A text message from an unknown number flashed on the screen:

"Walk away, Grayson. Or you'll vanish next."

Elliot's heart pounded. His entire body ached, but adrenaline pushed him forward. He stumbled out of the freight yard, gripping his injured shoulder.

He needed help. Fast.

Dialing a number, he put the phone to his ear. "I need an extraction. Now."

The voice on the other end sighed. "I told you to drop this, Elliot."

"They took Langston. I just watched them—"

"Doesn't matter," the voice interrupted. "You were warned. Get out while you still can."

The line went dead.

Elliot cursed under his breath. He had come too far. He wasn't going to stop now.

As he reached the street, headlights flooded his vision. A black car screeched to a halt in front of him. The window rolled down just enough for Elliot to see a gloved hand holding a piece of paper.

He hesitated. Then, slowly, he took it.

The car sped off before he could react.

Elliot unfolded the note, his blood running cold at the words scrawled across the paper:

"Project Obsidian isn't just erasing trials. They're rewriting reality."

19

The Ultimate Cover-Up

Elliot Grayson's breath came in sharp bursts as he crouched behind an overturned metal crate, his heart hammering against his ribs. The air in the abandoned shipping yard was thick with the acrid scent of burnt rubber, the echo of gunfire still ringing in his ears. He clutched the burner phone tighter, Carter Langston's voice still fresh in his mind.

"You think you know the truth? You have no idea."

The words reverberated in his skull as he risked a glance over the edge of the crate. The men in tactical gear had fanned out, their movements synchronized and precise. Whoever they were, they weren't ordinary operatives. They moved like ghosts, silent and efficient, their weapons raised and ready.

Elliot's mind worked frantically. If Langston was alive, then whose body had been found? More importantly, why had the government—or whoever was behind this—gone through such lengths to erase every trace of the trial?

A sharp whistle pierced the silence. Elliot turned just in time to see a dark figure gesturing at him from behind a stack of shipping containers. He hesitated for only a second

77

before sprinting toward the shadows. Bullets zipped past him, ricocheting off metal and concrete. His lungs burned as he dove behind the container, rolling to his side.

"Keep your head down," a low voice hissed.

Elliot turned to face his unlikely savior. Dr. Thomas Bell. The neuroscientist who had warned him about memory hacking. His clothes were disheveled, his face lined with exhaustion.

"What the hell are you doing here?" Elliot whispered.

Bell didn't answer immediately. He pulled a device from his pocket—a small black cylinder with a blinking red light. He pressed a button, and suddenly, all the gunfire ceased. The tactical team froze in place, their movements jerky, as if fighting an unseen force.

"EMP disruptor," Bell explained quickly. "Short-range, fries their comms and targeting systems. Won't last long."

Elliot's eyes widened. "You planned this?"

Bell shook his head. "No. I came to warn you. We have to move. Now."

They wove through the labyrinth of containers, reaching a rusted service door. Bell jammed a keycard against the scanner, and the lock clicked open. Elliot followed him inside, the darkness swallowing them whole.

"How did you find me?" Elliot asked, panting.

"You weren't exactly subtle," Bell replied. "After your last broadcast, I knew they'd come for you. I've been tracking their movements. They're not just erasing trials, Elliot. They're rewriting history itself."

Elliot exhaled sharply. "Project Obsidian."

Bell's face darkened. "You found the files. Good. That means we might still have a chance."

They emerged in a dimly lit corridor lined with rusted pipes.

Bell led the way, his footsteps eerily silent.

"Where are we?" Elliot asked.

"An old government warehouse. One of many. They use sites like this to store things they don't want found. Evidence, records, people." Bell's voice was grim. "And if we're not careful, we'll end up in one of their files."

A metallic clang echoed behind them. Bell grabbed Elliot's arm and yanked him into a side room. They pressed against the wall as footsteps neared. Shadows stretched across the doorway. Elliot held his breath, fingers inching toward the pocketknife in his jacket.

Then, just as suddenly, the footsteps retreated.

Bell exhaled. "We need to get to the main server room. If we can access their database, we can expose everything."

Elliot's pulse quickened. "And how exactly do we do that without getting killed?"

Bell smirked. "With a little help."

He pulled out a battered radio and pressed a button. "We're in. Move to Phase Two."

A crackle of static, then a voice Elliot didn't recognize: "Acknowledged. Stand by."

Before Elliot could question him, a series of explosions rocked the facility. Sirens wailed, and emergency lights flickered to life. Bell grabbed his wrist. "That's our distraction. Let's go."

They sprinted down the hallway, ducking past guards scrambling to respond to the breach. The deeper they went, the colder the air became. Finally, Bell stopped before a heavy steel door.

"This is it," he said. "The mainframe is behind this door. Everything they've deleted, every erased record, every altered event—it's all stored here."

Elliot's hands trembled. "How do we get inside?"

Bell gestured to a retinal scanner. "We need an authorized scan. And I have just the thing."

From his bag, he pulled a small vial filled with a viscous red liquid. "Synthetic ocular replication. A perfect copy of an authorized eye scan."

Elliot's stomach churned. "Whose eye?"

Bell didn't answer. He simply lifted the vial to the scanner. The machine whirred, then beeped. "Access granted."

The door slid open. Inside, rows upon rows of servers hummed, their blinking lights casting eerie reflections on the glass panels. Elliot stepped inside, overwhelmed by the sheer magnitude of it all.

Bell hurried to a terminal, plugging in a portable drive. "Once I decrypt the files, we send everything to the press, the courts—hell, even the United Nations if we have to."

Elliot nodded, wiping sweat from his brow. "Do it."

The screen flickered. Lines of code scrolled at dizzying speed. Bell's fingers flew across the keyboard. "Almost there..."

Then the alarms changed. A new sound. Deeper. More urgent.

Bell cursed. "They know we're here."

Elliot turned to the doorway. Shadows moved beyond the glass walls. "We need to hurry."

Bell hit a final key. "Done! The files are transferring."

The door burst open. Armed men flooded the room. Elliot raised his hands as Bell stepped forward, hands in the air.

A man in a crisp black suit entered. He moved with quiet authority, his face an unreadable mask.

"Elliot Grayson," the man said smoothly. "Dr. Bell. You've been very busy."

Elliot's jaw tightened. "Who are you?"

The man smiled faintly. "Call me Mr. Vance. And I'm afraid

this is where your investigation ends."

Bell lunged for the keyboard. A gunshot rang out. He staggered, clutching his side, blood seeping through his fingers.

Elliot shouted, catching Bell as he fell. The files! The upload—

A second shot. Pain exploded in Elliot's skull. His vision blurred, then faded to black.

The last thing he heard before losing consciousness was Vance's voice:

"Erase them both."

20

The Verdict That Never Happened

The cold, damp air in the interrogation room pressed against Elliot's skin like an iron shackle. He blinked against the harsh fluorescent light above, its flickering glow casting shadows on the pale gray walls. His wrists burned where the handcuffs bit into his skin, his pulse thrumming with a mixture of fear and defiance. Across from him, a shadowed figure leaned forward, their voice smooth and devoid of emotion.

"You know too much."

Elliot swallowed hard, his mind racing. His last memory before waking up here was the deafening silence of the abandoned courthouse basement, the sealed files labeled 'Project Obsidian'—the undeniable proof that someone, somewhere, had rewritten history.

A door creaked open. Heavy footsteps echoed off the walls. A second figure entered the room, their presence radiating authority. The air thickened with unspoken menace.

"Mr. Grayson," the second figure said, his voice gravelly, deliberate. "You're persistent. That's an admirable trait. Unfortunately, it's also a dangerous one."

Elliot lifted his chin. "The truth is dangerous to those trying to bury it."

The man chuckled, a sound devoid of amusement. He stepped into the light, revealing piercing gray eyes and a sharp jawline. "You have no idea what truth even looks like anymore, do you?"

Elliot remained silent. He had spent weeks piecing together fragments of a puzzle designed to be unsolvable. Carter Langston's vanished trial, the erased judge, the Blackout Files, the secret syndicate—each clue leading him deeper into a labyrinth of deceit.

The man placed a folder on the table and slid it toward Elliot. "Do you know what this is?"

Elliot didn't move. He could see the official insignia on the cover—an eagle, talons clutching a set of scales. Some faction of the government, buried so deep it didn't officially exist.

"Project Obsidian," the man confirmed, tapping a gloved finger against the folder. "A necessary intervention."

Elliot forced a smirk. "Erasing trials? Deleting verdicts? That's what you call 'necessary'?"

The man ignored his sarcasm. "Justice is an illusion, Mr. Grayson. People believe in it because they need to. But the world isn't fair. And sometimes, to maintain order, some cases must never exist."

Elliot's stomach twisted. "Who decides that?"

A silence stretched between them, heavy with implication.

"The people who keep the world from falling apart," the man finally said.

Elliot's pulse pounded in his ears. He thought of Judge Holloway, erased like she had never been born. Of the juror who had run, only to be silenced by a sniper's bullet. Of the journalist before him, Lisa Moreau, who had uncovered the truth and disappeared without a trace. And of Carter Langston, a billionaire whose trial had been wiped from history—yet whose corpse had surfaced under impossible circumstances.

The man flipped open the folder, revealing a stack of documents. Names. Dates. Transcripts of trials that never were.

Elliot's breath hitched. There were dozens of them.

"Why show me this?" he asked, his voice hoarse.

The man smiled, but there was no warmth in it. "Because you have two choices, Mr. Grayson."

He leaned in, his presence suffocating.

"You walk away. You forget this story. You live."

Elliot swallowed, the metallic taste of dread coating his tongue. "And the second choice?"

The man's eyes darkened. "You join the people who vanished before you."

The words settled into Elliot's bones like lead. He thought of the files he had seen, the truth he had uncovered. If he let this go, if he walked away now, justice would remain a fantasy, manipulated by the unseen hands of power.

A sudden buzz cut through the tension. The man's earpiece crackled, a voice murmuring something Elliot couldn't hear. The man's expression tightened.

"We're out of time," he muttered, standing abruptly. "Decide, Grayson. Now."

The lights flickered. A distant alarm blared through the corridors.

Then—darkness.

A sharp bang echoed, followed by the unmistakable sound of a scuffle. A body hit the floor. Elliot yanked at his restraints, his heartbeat hammering in his ears. Footsteps approached in the darkness, then—click—a flashlight beam illuminated his face.

"Elliot."

A familiar voice.

His breath caught. "Lisa?"

She didn't answer. She pulled a small device from her pocket and pressed it against the lock on his cuffs. A sharp beep, then the metal restraints snapped open.

"We have to move," she said, gripping his arm and hauling him to his feet.

Elliot's mind reeled. Lisa Moreau had disappeared five years ago. He had seen the last words she ever wrote. And yet, here she was, leading him through the darkness of the facility like a ghost resurrected.

"Wait—how—"

"No time," she cut in. "They'll be back any second."

Gunfire erupted in the distance. Lisa shoved him against the wall just as another door burst open. A silhouette appeared in the emergency lighting, raising a weapon.

Lisa fired first.

The guard dropped without a sound.

Elliot's chest heaved. "You—"

She grabbed his wrist and pulled him forward. "Move!"

They tore through the corridors, alarms screeching around them. Elliot's thoughts spun. Project Obsidian. The erased trials. The people who had been made to disappear. Lisa. Was she one of them? Had she escaped? Or had she been playing a different game all along?

As they neared an exit, Lisa pulled out a phone and tossed it to him. "Everything you need is on there."

He caught it, his fingers tightening around the device. "Where are we going?"

"We're not," she said, yanking open a maintenance hatch.

"You go. I stay."

Elliot froze. "No—"

Lisa's expression softened. "You need to tell the world. Someone has to."

A surge of voices and footsteps pounded toward them. Lisa pushed him through the hatch. "Run, Elliot. Don't stop."

And then—

The door slammed shut between them.

Elliot stumbled into the night air, his mind screaming in protest. Behind him, chaos erupted. He ran, the cold biting into his skin, his pulse thundering.

He didn't stop.

He didn't look back.

Lisa had just handed him the most dangerous secret in modern history.

And now, it was up to him to expose it.